C000030107

WELCOME

This commemorative magazine has been published to celebrate the life and career of England's greatest living footballer - Sir Tom Finney.

It is packed full of photographs and memorabilia that trace Sir Tom's illustrious career from the pre-war years to the present day.

Magnificent tributes spill out from every page written by some of the most influential people in football as well as admirers and fans going back many generations.

We believe that this magazine draws a simple conclusion 'Sir Tom Finney is a truly remarkable human being who throughout his life has brought great credit to his family, the City of Preston and the game of football'

I am so very proud to call him my friend

Jim Cadman

CONTENTS

Sir Tom Finney
Commemorative Magazine

First published in the UK
by Football Heroes Publishing in 2008
County Lane, Stourbridge, West Midlands DY8 2SB.

ISBN 978-0-9560756-0-4

Copyright © Football Heroes Publishing 2008
Publication concept devised and created by Jim Cadman. All rights reserved Copyright © Jim Cadman 2008.

The rights of the contributors has been asserted in accordance with the Copyright, Designs and Patents Act 1998.

The publisher and contributors have made every effort to contact all copyright holders. Any errors that may have been occurred are inadvertent and anyone who for any reason has not been contacted is invited to write to the publisher so that a full acknowledgement can be made in subsequent editions of this magazine.

The publishers would like to thank the following people and organisations who, without their input, this publication would not have been possible.

Contributors
Sir Tom Finney, Jim Cadman, Tom Roe, Paul Burns, Ian Rigby, Mike Payne, Ben Rose, The Mall Preston, Guild Hall Preston, Preston City Council, Preston North End FC, Lancashire County Council, National Football Museum.

Design and Artwork
© Paul Burns, Crown Creative Limited
Tel: 01384 274 774
paul.burns@crowncreative.co.uk

Printing
Printed and bound by Paper Innovation Ltd
Tel: 01772 562 526
www.paperinnovation.co.uk

Photography and Images
© Sir Tom Finney family, PA Photos, Getty Images, Jim Cadman, Tom Roe, Ian Rigby, National Football Museum, Howard Talbot, LEP, Action Images, Preston North End FC, Westmoreland Gazette, David Foster.

recycle

GENUINE STANDARD
RUBSTUDS
REGISTERED AND PATENTED
COMPLY IN EVERY RESPECT WITH F.A. LAW 4 (Revised)

Recommended by

and many other leading internationals

THE ULTIMATE TEAM PLAYER

"Sir Tom Finney not only helped define Preston North End as a football club, he also defined the town and, in many ways, an era of football."

Sir David Richards,
Chairman, The Premier League

His style of play - marrying skill, flair and pace to a work ethic and an appreciation that football is ultimately best played as a team - would have seen him excel in any given decade of the modern game. Bill Shankly, never one to deliver undeserving praise, described him as 'the greatest player I ever saw in all my time'.

Premier League managers would salivate at the prospect of such a talent and Tom would be able to name his price - something he resolutely refused to do as he gave unstinting service to PNE.

"Premier League managers would salivate at the prospect of such a talent and Tom would be able to name his price"

That his playing career is so heralded to this day is made all the more remarkable by the fact he never won any major trophies as a player. It was Tom's play and attitude that captivated the imagination and enduring accolades that he so richly deserves. It was recognised during his heyday with PNE and England when he was voted Footballer of the Year both in 1954 and 1957 and I am delighted that we are being given the opportunity to reflect on the achievements of a man who Bobby Moore described as 'the last great England winger'.

SIR DAVID RICHARDS,
CHAIRMAN, THE PREMIER LEAGUE

THE PERFECT ROLE MODEL

"In this day and age when it has become part of the territory for a professional footballer to be very mindful of the impact that he has on youngsters taking part in the game, it is very appropriate to remind ourselves of the likes of Sir Tom Finney who epitomised the very essence of a role model, not only for young footballers but for young people everywhere, both throughout his career and since his magnificent career ended in the way that he has been an excellent ambassador for his home town, Preston, and for football in general."

Gordon Taylor, Chief Executive
The Professional Footballers' Association

On becoming chairman of the PFA in 1978, I was delighted to convince the management committee at that time to give Sir Tom a special merit award and enter him into the PFA's Hall of Fame for his contribution to football at my first awards dinner as chairman. Since then, of course, Preston has become synonymous with the National Football Museum and their Hall of Fame respecting other great contributors to our game but Sir Tom still remains at the pinnacle.

Born in 1944 in Ashton under Lyne, near Manchester, the 50's became a time when all of us local lads who were football daft recreated our heroes on the local spare ground and cup finals were always the special event of the year. In 1954, just like the year before, all our fingers were crossed that Sir Tom would get a cup winners medal although it was not to be like his great contemporary, Sir Stanley Matthews, the year before. He featured regularly in Charles Buchan's Soccer Monthly and the Annual Soccer Gift Book when it was all our ambitions to get as many autographs as possible and, needless to say, Tom was always willing to give his autograph. You can imagine how I felt, having been successful with the town schoolboy team and Lancashire Schoolboys having had a trial for England, I was approached by a number of clubs including Preston North End when Cliff Brittain was the manager and George Barge was the scout for the club and invited myself, my dad and my uncle over to Preston for Sir Tom's last game against Luton Town. Imagine my utter delight when the manager went into the dressing room and brought Sir Tom out to meet me, who on probably one of the most emotional days of his career, took the time to have a good chat with me all about professional football and wished me all the best. Such a meeting has left an indelible memory for me and summarised Sir Tom perfectly that even though he was the biggest star in the game he always had time for everybody including the latest possible new recruit.

I consider it one of the finest privileges of my life to know Sir Tom, to call him a friend and to be able to pay tribute to his great qualities and the fact that he has always been willing to support the Professional Footballers' Association. It was fantastic to have him part of our centenary celebrations last year along with the other Knights of football to make our centenary night a magnificent celebration of all that has been good in football and to make me feel proud as he undoubtedly has made all the population of Preston very proud to call him their own.

GORDON TAYLOR
CHIEF EXECUTIVE, THE PFA

MODESTY IS HIS MIDDLE NAME

"For those of us who never had the privilege of watching Sir Tom Finney play, meeting the great man is the next best thing.
Hearing Sir Tom talk about the 'golden era' of English football after the War, when the England team brimmed with entertainers, is a wonderful privilege."

Henry Winter, Daily Telegraph football correspondent

Sir Tom believes that in an age of rationing and austerity footballers felt a duty to put on a show, to splash some colour onto the monochrome canvas of post-War life. When England took on Italy in 1948, Finney and Stanley Matthews certainly let rip, zigzagging this way and that, leaving their full-backs with legs like twisted tagliatelli.

Finney even scored twice. "That game gave me a great thrill," Sir Tom recalls of the 4-0 victory. "Italy were world champions. The Italians were really surprised England played so well."

Finney's name is revered today because of his loyalty to Preston North End and his 30 goals in 76 England internationals between 1946 and 1958. And for so much more. Finney will forever be associated with fair play, for showing respect to an opponent, for dignity.

"Stan (Matthews) had the necessary know-how to beat men easily. I wondered how on earth he got that skill! I felt sorry for the defender!"

Sir Tom Finney

The true sporting greats are blessed with grace. Modesty should be Tom Finney's middle name. Anyone talking to Sir Tom about his contribution to those halcyon post-War days will find him directing praise elsewhere, to those other characters who made the England dressing room such a special place.

Even now, more than a half-century on, Finney's eyes light up at the memory of those he played alongside. "I always admired Stan, a great player," he reflects. "Stan had the necessary know-how to beat men easily. I wondered how on earth he got that skill! I felt sorry for the defender! We often used to say in the England side how difficult it must be as a defender playing against Stan!"

A dip into the FA archives confirm how Finney and Matthews tore opponents apart. "The first time the two played together for England they ran Portugal ragged, both men scoring in a 10-0 victory," reads the report in the official England history kept at Soho Square.

Other talents filled the England side. "Wilf Mannion was small, very good," adds Sir Tom. "He impressed me with his technique. Stan Mortensen was a character, a really good player to have in your side because he never knew when he was beaten. Nat Lofthouse was an outstanding centre-forward, very strong, very quick and good with his head. Nat was a great character off the pitch. He was always making fun of people in the dressing room! Mostly banter!

"It was a golden era. Jackie Milburn was very, very quick. In training, over 50 yards, he was the quickest thing I had ever seen. He was a very, very good player but he was nervous before a game. I have never seen a player that experienced so nervous prior to a game, particularly against foreigners, because you didn't really know much about them.

"Bobby Charlton was an up-and-coming star when I was finishing. He so impressed me. After seeing him for the first time, I knew he had the makings of an outstanding player. His ability stood out." So did Finney's. A celebration of Tom Finney's career is a celebration of the very greatest footballing virtues.

HENRY WINTER,
DAILY TELEGRAPH
FOOTBALL CORRESPONDENT

'The Preston Plumber'

Taking the first steps on the ladder of success as an England International footballer and a regular in the Preston North End First Team, but life must go on for Tom Finney as a Plumber and a working man.

Picture taken 1946

No.7 FOR THE NORTH END

"I made a point of going to watch Mr Finney whenever the North End came to London. Every minute was a privilege. It is safe to assume that the cloth-capped multitudes who saw Tom Finney play 433 matches for Preston in the 15 years from 1946 to 1960, scoring 187 goals along the way, felt the same."

Jeff Powell, chief sports feature writer, Daily Mail

When I was still a lad in short trousers my grandfather, who had played right back for Bury in their halcyon days, decided to further my education by taking me onto the North Bank at Highbury to see Arsenal play Preston.

Shortly before kick-off he hoisted me onto his shoulders with this instruction: "If you want to learn something about football forget about the game and just watch Mr Finney. He's the no.7 for the North End." And so I did, transfixed for 90 minutes. And so my eyes were opened to the genius of the man we are honouring here tonight, more than half a century later.

From that day on, I made a point of going to watch Mr Finney whenever the North End came to London. Every minute was a privilege. It is safe to assume that the cloth-capped multitudes who saw Tom Finney play 433 matches for Preston in the 15 years from 1946 to 1960, scoring 187 goals along the way, felt the same. What I did not know, until years later, was that this truly great man held no such exalted opinion of himself.

London was the venue for the first attempt to establish a Hall of Fame for our national game. Tom travelled down from Preston for the opening and, to my delight, I found myself standing next to him as we watched simultaneous film of famous matches from different eras.

"What do you think?" I asked, after introducing myself. "Well, a bit embarrassed really," he replied, coughing shyly. "I mean, the game was so much slower in my day."

At that moment a sepia image of Tom sprinting and shimmying past three defenders before scoring with a cross-shot of characteristic precision flickered across one of the screens. "Mr Finney," I said, "if you were playing now you would be just as quick, but also a darned sight cleverer than any of our modern players... and doing exactly what we have just seen you do on that film."

What Tom did not do, was earn the £100,000 a week he would have commanded now.

A personally signed photo and programme to Tom from Field Marshall Montgomery after watching Finney score England's first goal against Scotland at Hampden Park 1948

Fourteen quid a week was his lot, 14 good reasons why he kept working as a plumber and kept travelling by bus to Deepdale, the ground near which he was born on April 5th, 1922.

You can't buy loyalty and, unlike today's £30m transfer men, Finney is the ultimate one-club man. Fame and fortune matter nothing to him. Friendship and the genuine respect of his fellow man mean everything. Although the start of his earnings career was delayed until he was 24, while he answered a more urgent call from his country by fighting with Montgomery's Eighth Army in North Africa, he later declined the chance to bank a comparative fortune by transferring to Italy.

Tom's value to the North End is not registered in trophies and medals. No, the immensity of his contribution to a club woven into the folklore of our football is to be found in the disparity of Preston's performances without him.

In both his first two League seasons they finished seventh and reached the quarter finals of the FA Cup. The following season they were well up the first division until he was injured, then relegated in his absence.

A year later, a fit-again Finney led them back up to the top flight and it was not long before they were being pipped to the championship by Arsenal one season, then narrowly beaten by West Bromwich Albion in the Cup Final the next.

When he retired in 1960, aged 36, he left Preston in ninth place. The following season they were relegated without him and now, at 86 and as their Life President, Sir Tom Finney still loyally awaits their return to the top flight. Through it all, the legend of Finney the England wizard lives on.

Ask this perfect English gentleman who might be the best footballer ever to play for his country and he answers: "Oh, that would be Stan."

> *"If you are as good as Tom Finney was, you don't have to tell anybody."*
>
> *Bobby Moore*

That, of course, would be Sir Stanley Matthews, his contemporary on the wing. So Finney leaves it to others to point out that he was the more complete player, as witnessed by the ease with which he made his frequent transitions to centre forward.

Matthews was the dribbler supreme, but Finney was more than just a mesmerising talent on the ball. By moving inside to score even more goals in the physically challenging no.9 position, Finney demonstrated wider powers of adaptablity as well as higher echelons of courage.

Nothing becomes a true superstar more than his modesty. As Bobby Moore once told me when we were discussing Tom's place in the pantheon of the game: "If you are as good as Tom Finney was, you don't have to tell anybody."

English football's 'Hall of Fame' now resides in its proud and proper place. Where else but the birthplace and lifelong home of the Preston Plumber, Sir Thomas Finney, the greatest English footballer of them all.

JEFF POWELL,
CHIEF SPORTS FEATURE WRITER, DAILY MAIL

Finney with an array of awards, caps, medals and trophies he accumulated over his career.

FERRARIS | COUNTRY HOUSE, HOTEL AND RESTAURANT

THE HOTEL HAS 22 INDIVIDUALLY DESIGNED EN-SUITE
BEDROOMS RANGING FROM COSY STANDARD ROOMS TO DELUXE
BEDROOMS.

WEDDINGS AND PRIVATE CEREMONIES CATERING FOR 20 TO 200 GUESTS.

FERRARIS IS ALSO FULLY LICENSED FOR CIVIL CEREMONIES.

FOR FURTHER DETAILS PLEASE CONTACT: 01772 783148 OR EMAIL
INFO@FERRARISCOUNTRYHOUSE.CO.UK

WWW.FERRARISCOUNTRYHOUSE.CO.UK

FERRARIS COUNTRY HOUSE HOTEL & RESTAURANT, CHIPPING LANE, THORNLEY, LONGRIDGE, PRESTON PR3 2TB

A VALUABLE BLUEPRINT FOR THE YOUNG PLAYERS OF TODAY

"It is a great honour to be asked to contribute a few words here about Sir Tom Finney - a man held in the highest esteem and affection by everybody at Arsenal Football Club."

Peter Hill-Wood, Chairman, Arsenal FC

Above: Tom Finney and William Dodgin at Deepdale

It has also been pointed out to me that he scored four times against Arsenal in the 1956/57 season - still thrilling crowds with his grace, control and finishing into his 34th year.

Sir Tom and Arsenal also share an important influence - that of Alex James. The Scotsman was a true star both for Preston North End and the Gunners, and I know that Sir Tom has often spoken of the profound influence that Alex and his mesmerising style had on his own game while watching him at a young age.

It remains for me to congratulate Sir Tom on a very special, and richly-deserved, occasion. Alongside his remarkable footballing ability, his acute values of sportsmanship, dignity and love for the game have enriched all of us who hold football dear and provide a valuable blueprint for any young player starting out today. We are proud to call him a friend.

PETER HILL-WOOD,
CHAIRMAN, ARSENAL FC

Sir Tom's and Arsenal's fates were intertwined memorably on occasion and these times certainly bear recollection. As a promising 19-year-old, a young Tom was pitched into Preston's side to face us in the Final of the 1941 wartime cup, in which he set up his team's goal in a 1-1 draw. Preston won the ensuing replay 2-1 and already it was clear that a future star was born. One cannot help but wonder what he and his team mates of the early 1940s might have achieved together in first-class football had war not intervened.

Perhaps our most momentous meetings with Sir Tom came in the 1952/53 season, when our two clubs fought out what must be the closest title race in history. Sir Tom scored at Highbury in a 1-1 draw, and then repeated the feat at Deepdale on the penultimate day of the season. Preston won that game 2-0, leaving us both neck and neck going into the final game. History shows that Arsenal beat Burnley a week later to win the league on goal average, but the efforts of a fine Preston side that surely deserved a title of its own during the 1950s cannot be forgotten.

MY GREAT FRIEND, THE LEGEND STANLEY MATTHEWS

"Stanley Matthews was without any shadow of doubt a footballing genius. He was an incredible entertainer, a wing wizard with the ball who the fans on the terraces absolutely adored."

Sir Tom Finney

Stan and I were close and shared a mutual respect both on and off the football field. I was often left in awe at his skill and his professionalism, after all you don't continue playing football at a professional at 50-years-old unless you have dedicated your life to rigorous exercise and a spartan diet.

When I broke into the England team Stan was already an established international, recognised throughout the world as a player with a God given gift. He was brilliant, a pleasure to play alongside and to watch.

Stan was the greatest ball player of his generation, who showed no mercy to defenders as he moved past them with ease as the ball remained attached to his boot as if by sheer magic. He would drop his shoulder, wiggle his hips and move with the defender left stranded in a trance like state.

"I often reflect on my career and think that if I could be born again as any other player I would have chosen to be Stanley Matthews."

England called on the services of Stanley Matthews as an international 54 times over a period of 23 years and he was still playing for Stoke City at 50-years-old having made a total of 697 league appearances for Blackpool and Stoke.

I considered Stan to be a great friend and I was honoured to be one of a quartet of men chosen to provide a guard of honour for his funeral at St Peter Ad Vincula Church in Stoke on Trent on Friday 3rd March 2000.

I often reflect on my career and think that if I could be born again as any other player I would have chosen to be Stanley Matthews.

DID YOU KNOW?

Matthews won the inaugural Football Writers' Association Footballer of the Year award in 1948.

In 1956, Matthews won the first-ever European Footballer of the Year (Balon d'Or) award, and the following year was awarded a CBE.

In 1961 (aged 46) he rejoined his home town club, Stoke City. The following season, Stoke City won the Second Division Championship and he was voted Footballer of the Year for the second time in his career.

In 1965, he became the first football player to be knighted for services to sport. He received a FIFA Gold Merit Order in 1992.

Matthews remained with Stoke City until the end of his playing career, appearing in his final game on February 6th 1965, just after his 50th birthday! In later years he always claimed he had retired 'too early'.

> "Tom Finney would have been great in any team, in any match and in any age."

BILL SHANKLY

A LEGEND IS BORN

And it came to pass that Tom Finney was just one of six young debutants in the opening game of the 1940/41 Wartime season.

The Preston North End club policy at that time was to use their own players, whenever possible, however inexperienced, rather than depend on 'guest players'. In the Liverpool line-up that afternoon was goalkeeper Sam Bartram (Charlton Athletic), Stan Cullis (Wolverhampton Wanderers) and former North Ender, Frank O'Donnell (Aston Villa). Liverpool legends Bob Paisley and Billy Liddell also played against the young Preston side that day so a 3-3 draw was an excellent result. The local newspaper actually called the young Preston players 'the babes', 18 years before the 'Busby Babes' became a well known saying! Finney was involved with two of the goals that afternoon, a good start to his career.

Tom's first 'home' game of his career was actually played at the nearby Leyland Motors ground, as Deepdale was closed, occupied by the Military initially as a 'reception centre'. In total, North End

played nine games at Leyland before Deepdale was partially re-opened on the 8th February 1941, for a game against Sheffield United. The old West Stand on Deepdale Road was closed until 1946. Admission prices at the ground were 1/1d on the ground (five pence) with juveniles and

Above: Preston North End FC 1939/1940.
Left: A programme from 1938 highlighting a young Tom Finney playing for the Preston Juniors 'B' team against the Preston Juniors 'A' team.

Preston North End FC War Cup Final Winners 1940/41.

*A programme from Christmas Day 1941
against Blackburn Rovers.*

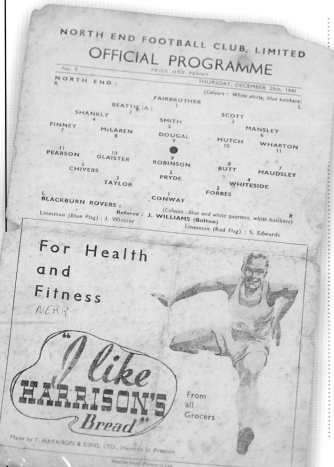

HM Forces in uniform being charged 7d. The dearest tickets were seats in the Pavilion Stand at 2/6d (12 1/2d). Finney apparently showed some delightful touches and thrilled the crowd with good approach play. His displays from the onset of the season brought about the following write up from 'Perseus' of the Lancashire Evening Post (15th February 1941).

A Star in the making

When I first saw him, I wrote warmly of the qualities of young Finney and I wanted to see how right I was in that judgement. My thoughts were fully warranted, and I repeat that he has the makings of the finest outside-right I have seen since Stanley Matthews. The boy's gifts are those of a ripe, experienced player. He doesn't yet know, of course, how always to apply them to the maximum advantage. That will come with experience. He can slip like an eel between two opponents, with the ball under perfect control. What is quite uncommon is his sense of timing, which is always the difference between the good player and the star. His left foot is refreshing. We shall hear more of Finney, that I am sure.

On the same day as this brilliant prophecy was printed Preston North End started their War Cup run with a game against Bury at Gigg Lane. Finney scored twice in a 4-4 draw and was praised as the most effective and polished of the Preston forward line.

THE WAR CUP FINAL

Having disposed of Bury (6-5), Bolton Wanderers (6-1), Tranmere Rovers (20-2), Manchester City (5-1) and Newcastle United (2-0) in two-legged games, Preston North End earned the right to play Arsenal in the 1940/41 War Cup Final, at Wembley.

This was to be the first of many appearances at Wembley for Tom Finney. Going into the final on May 10th, Preston had been unbeaten since late December, scoring 60 goals and only conceding 15 along the way. Unfortunately, due to the bombings, fewer than 200 fans travelled by train to London. No special coaches were available either due to the petrol rationing. The game ended in a 1-1 draw so the replay, to be fair to the fans, had to be fairly local. Eventually Ewood Park, Blackburn, was preferred to Liverpool's Anfield ground. Preston North End only received 600 of the cheaper five shilling and six pence tickets, but had 7,000 applications. In all, the Club got less than 5,000 tickets.

On the day of the replay (31st May) the queues started forming around 10 am and a military band played to the happy crowd. On a sad note, the Mayor of Blackburn, Walter Tempest, who was also Blackburn Rovers' chairman, had died during that week. It was estimated that 10,000 football fans from around the 'banks of the Ribble' cheered the teams to the field. Finney made many dazzling runs but to no avail as the teams, once again cancelled each other out. Three minutes after half-time, Finney collected a good ball from Andy Beattie and quickly squared it to Jimmy Dougal, who in turn slipped it onto Bobbie Beattie to score. Arsenal scored through an own goal but whilst still celebrating, Beattie, straight from the kick-off scored his and Preston's second goal to win the cup. Preston North End were dubbed the 'team of the season' in English football. Finney was one of six players pointed out for special praise by the press. Cultured football had won the day.

Now for the double

A midweek defeat by Blackpool (cup hangover!) made Preston more determined to win the League, and with it the 'double', with a victory on the last day of the season, versus Liverpool. Straight from the whistle the Finney/McLaren wing partnership looked sharp and lively. Finney helped set up the game's first three goals, all scored by McLaren, and just before half-time McLaren made it 4-0 from a Beattie pass. Finney's duel with full-back Jackson was an engaging feature of the game with Finney bringing applause from the Deepdale fans on numerous occasions. McLaren went on to score a double hat-trick in a 6-1 demolition of Liverpool on the day that the Club did the League and War Cup Final double. It was a grand finale to a grand season, a sumptuous exhibition of attacking flair by a Preston team on top of their game, with a blend of youth, experience and a new emerging star of the future in their midst.

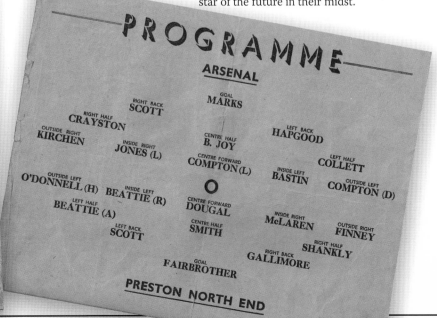

Steady... Aim... FIRE!

Finney sends a bullet shot from distance against
Charlton Athletic at Deepdale in 1953

WHAT A RECORD

	APPEARANCES	GOALS
Preston North End - League	433	187
Preston North End - FA Cup	40	23
England - Internationals	76	30
The Football League	17	7
Total	**566**	**247**

FACTS

Scored on his debuts at outside-right, outside-left and centre-forward for England.

Scored on his debuts for Preston in all five forward positions.

Scored on both his North End debut and his England debut.

Made 71 appearances in Division Two and scored 23 goals.

Had his best run of consecutive appearances, 29, in 1950/51.

Once scored in eight consecutive appearances for PNE, in 1957/58.

Played in 21 countries for England and against 23 different countries.

Never scored a hat-trick for Preston but did score four for England in one game, against Portugal.

Scored 26 league goals in 1957/58, his best total.

Scored 28 league and cup goals in 1956/57, his best for a season.

Missed 11 penalties for Preston but scored from 35.

Worst run without scoring was 12 games in 1949/50.

Scored against 42 different teams in the league.

Best total against one team was 11 against Manchester City.

Also scored ten goals each against Portsmouth, Sheffield Wed. and Bolton.

Scored most penalties against Spurs and Bolton (four each).

Scored six goals for England against Portugal and five against Wales.

Set an England scoring record with 30 goals.

Was elected Footballer of the Year twice, the first person to gain such recognition.
His awards came in 1954 and 1957.

Wrote two books, Finney on Football and Football Around the World.

Once had a play written about his life and it was performed in the city.

Won a Second Division Champions medal in 1950/51.

Won a League Championship runners-up medal twice, in 1953 and 1958.

Won an FA Cup runners-up medal in 1953/54.

Appeared at Wembley in 16 internationals, one FA Cup Final
and one Wartime Cup Final.

Was awarded the OBE in 1961.

Was made a Freeman of Preston in 1967.

Was awarded the CBE in 1992.

Was Knighted at Buckingham Palace in 1998.

Was inducted into the National Football Museum's
Hall of Fame in 2002.

Is the current Preston North End President.

Finney's statue, replicating the famous image of 'The Splash'
is in front of the ground.

Finney's face was built into the seats of the new stand,
opened in 1996, and called the Tom Finney Stand.

FINNEY'S LEAGUE DEBUT

After serving his country in the Army his long awaited league debut was at Deepdale against Leeds United on 31st August 1946.

It cost one shilling and three pence to stand on the Spion Kop in those days but an expensive seven shillings and six pence to sit in the Pavilion Stand. After just four minutes of the new season Tom Finney's enthusiastic run finished with his deadly accurate pass being turned past Hodgson's reach by debutant Willie McIntosh. The games second goal on 18 minutes, had class written all over it, with Finney, the schemer and scorer, showing that he was going to be a tremendous force in North End football. He had Milburn, the full-back, twisting and turning, baffled and leg-locked, as he unbalanced his opponent before making space and planting a beautiful shot just inside the post. Storming applause greeted this solo effort. His first of many goals for PNE. Milburn incurred the referee's displeasure as he fouled Finney repeatedly but Tom was delighting the crowd. Few could wish to be in a full-backs boots facing Finney on this form. He provided fascinating entertainment. To find a talent like Finney was rare. He excelled in his first game since being 'demobbed', His composure, artistry and tantalising finesse made his match-winning performance the talk of the town.

Versus Charlton Athletic 14th September 1946

Heavy rain kept many fans away as PNE took on the FA cup finalists, Charlton Athletic. Finney could play on any surface and so it proved in this game. Only a few minutes had elapsed when he skipped along the bye line and broke free of his marker to set up George Mutch for the games first goal. Finney continued to dazzle in the early stages as he harassed his marker, Shreeve, into submission. From a Finney centre McIntosh doubled the score and soon made it 3-0. Both McIntosh & Mutch scored again in the second half but it was Finney who received the plaudits. "He is great because he is so different" wrote Viator of the LEP, "always adapting his repertoire of tricks and finesse to the opportunity and rarely wastes the ball."

September 18th 1946

England International trial match at Nottingham Stan Matthews was injured so Tom got called up for his first international trial match but he was so starved of the ball he had hardly any chance to show his real ability. He was picked as a travelling reserve.

Return game versus Leeds United
28th December 1946

Next to an afternoon off, North End could not have wished for a more tranquil end to the Christmas period, earning seven points out of a possible eight. They were fifth in the league. Superlatives on Finney have long since been exhausted but sufficient to say, he was in a most dazzling mood. Even allowing for the deficiencies of the Leeds rearguard, this was the best right-wing display for weeks. The Elland Road crowd gave him generous applause for his marvellous display 'Aramis'.

May 10th 1946 versus Manchester United

Finney played a deep, studious game but Aston could not handle him as Finney was brilliant in all he did. Unfortunately, many of Finney's openings were wasted, hence the 1-1 scoreline.

Sports Goods for Every Sport

PRESTON SPORTS DEPOT

141 FRIARGATE PRESTON

TOM FINNEY
(ENGLAND and P.N.E.F.C.)

TEL 3793

FINNEY ON TOP FORM

Tom Finney, on top form, helped Preston North End equal a Football League record during this season. The team won 14 consecutive league games, starting at Christmas going right through to Easter.

25th	December	1950	4-1	away	vs	Queens Park Rangers
26th	December	1950	1-0	home	vs	Queens Park Rangers
30th	December	1950	2-0	away	vs	Cardiff City
13th	January	1951	1-0	home	vs	Birmingham City
20th	January	1951	4-0	away	vs	Grimsby Town
3rd	February	1951	3-1	home	vs	Notts. County
17th	February	1951	4-2	away	vs	Brentford
24th	February	1951	1-0	home	vs	Luton Town
3rd	March	1951	3-0	away	vs	Leeds United
10th	March	1951	7-0	home	vs	Barnsley
17th	March	1951	3-2	away	vs	Sheffield United
24th	March	1951	3-0	home	vs	Blackburn Rovers
26th	March	1951	3-2	home	vs	Leicester City
27th	March	1951	3-2	away	vs	Leicester City

25th December 1950. 4-1 away vs QPR
Unbelievably the headline was 'Finney, Wayman matchwinners' even though it was Charlie Wayman who scored all four goals. Having said that, all four goals came from crosses supplied by Tom Finney. He toyed with an insecure defence at will, causing havoc whenever he had possession of the ball. Wayman's opening goal was a back header.

3rd February 1951. 3-1 home vs Notts County
It took just six minutes to put the league leaders (PNE) ahead, a three-man move finished by Finney. Wayman sent Ken Horton away, but just as he released the perfect pass to Finney he was unceremoniously flattened. Having the advantage, Finney's first time shot flew unerringly into the far corner of the goal unseen by Horton who lay bleeding on the ground. Finney continued to tease and trick the County defenders, creating numerous chances. Despite being second best, the visitors managed to equalise against the run of play but North End soon regained the lead, just before half-time, playing superb 'on the carpet' football. Morrison putting the finishing touches to a great move. Apparently Finney was dangerous every time he gained possession of the ball. Defenders Simpson and Corkhill could not make up their minds as to which way Finney would turn next. Completely baffled, a further goal from Wayman finished them off. Preston North End were now four points ahead of challengers Manchester City, Blackburn Rovers, Coventry City and Cardiff City.

17th February 1951. 4-2 away vs Brentford
After 14 days of continuous rain it was touch and go

as to whether this game would actually start, never mind finish. The pitch was a quagmire, a sorry state of affairs, heavily sanded with sparse waterlogged grass in the corners. Even the coin was lost in the mud at the toss-up! The pitch demanded strength and stamina, not craft, but Finney had all of those in abundance. It was he who put North End ahead on 23 minutes, the reward for coolness and snap decision making. Bobbie Beattie, a born thinker and football artist in his own right, played him through, and although Tom was slipping in the mud, his first time shot surprised the goalkeeper. On 42 minutes Finney turned creator of a perfect second goal. Finding a rare dry patch, he sprinted in a 30-yard dash with the ball under amazing control before coolly laying on a chance for Horton to score. Finney was a constant menace and even the 'London press' raised their eyebrows in admiration. On 52 minutes Finney scored again, evading a certain penalty on the way, keeping his balance to score with a fast, well-placed shot. The crowd rose, showing their appreciation of a great player.

10th March 1951. 7-0 home vs Barnsley
Finney again was the matchwinner, his seemingly telepathic sense with Horton playing a great part in this victory. On 24 minutes, a quick one-two between them set the ball rolling, Finney side-stepping an incoming tackle prior to unleashing a great scoring shot. The promised goal avalanche soon materialised as Wayman and Horton added to the scoreline. Goal number four was down to Finney again as he leapt the highest in a packed goalmouth, and with perfect timing he nodded powerfully past the outstretched

hand of the goalkeeper. Everything was going well at Deepdale, the team was on fire so to speak, and after this 7-0 win promotion back to the top flight looked promising.

26th March 1951 3-2 home vs Leicester City

Tom Finney inspired the team to equal a Preston North End record of 13 consecutive wins with this latest victory on Easter Monday. Leicester caught North End napping with the 10.45 am morning kick-off taking a 1-0 lead into the half-time break. The second period produced different tactics though with North End upping their game to give a spirited display. Eventually Beattie found Finney clear of his 'watchdog' giving him the chance to cut in and set up Wayman for a deserved equaliser. Twenty minutes later a shot from Finney cannoned off a defender, straight to Wayman who notched his second goal of the game. North End completed a great recovery just eight minutes later when Finney scored a glorious solo goal which mirrored both his expert craftsmanship and his graceful purpose. Although the visitors caused a minor scare with a late penalty goal, Preston held onto the points and with them a very real chance of the Championship.

The following day the same two teams met at Filbert Street with Preston storming into a 3-0 lead in a 14 minute spell. A thrilling encounter ensued and despite a late rally from the 'Foxes' which produced two goals Preston shut up shop to record their 14th successive victory.

Although a 3-3 draw at Southampton ended the run of straight wins, the point won ensured promotion back to Division One, just two seasons after suffering relegation. The seven hour train journey back to Lancashire must have been an away day to remember for both players and fans alike.

Souvenir brochure celebrating Preston North End's Championship and promotion season.

Overleaf: The team that helped Preston North End win the Second Division Championship and promotion to the First Division.

PRESTON NORTH END F.C.
2nd. DIVISION CHAMPIONS · SEASON 1950-1951

T. FINNEY - PRESTON NORTH END

W. SCOTT - PRESTON NORTH END

W. CUNNINGHAM - PRESTON NORTH END

H. ANDERS - PRESTON NORTH END

T. DOCHERTY - PRESTON NORTH END

R. BEATTIE - PRESTON NORTH END

W. FORBES - PRESTON NORTH END

J. MARSTON - PRESTON NORTH END

E. QUIGLEY - PRESTON NORTH END

C. WAYMAN - PRESTON NORTH END

T. FINNEY and K. HORTON - PRESTON NORTH END

A. MORRISON - PRESTON NORTH END

J. GOOCH - PRESTON NORTH END

MY PERSONAL TRIBUTE TO THE REMARKABLE TOM FINNEY

"When I was asked to write about Sir Tom Finney for this special occasion I began to reflect on how many years I had known him. So I go back to Leyland Secondary Modern School when, as a young man, I was playing in a final of the Daily Despatch Shield and a young Preston player was going to present the Shield to the winners. That player was Tom Finney who was then 25 years of age."

Trevor J. Hemmings

From that day forward with my Father, Monty, who was a staunch Tom Finney fan, I used to go to watch the Preston team and enjoy the staggering standard of football that Tom was able to offer. In those days not only did you see the likes of Stanley Matthews playing against Preston, you also enjoyed watching many other Preston players including Bill Shankly, Tommy Docherty, Andy Beattie and Willie Cunningham all of whom were great friends of Tom. Within all of those names, Tom was unique in his football career earning 76 caps for his country.

I was always curious when so many people classed Tom as one of the finest footballers ever to grace the game. Now after many many years I know why and I am delighted to tell everyone else.

He is the only player I know in the world who has been selected for his country and played in all five forward positions, chosen four times in four different positions and, as for the fifth, an early injury to Raich Carter, an inside right for England, caused Tom to be

"Tom is always willing to chat to anyone whatever part of society they might be from. He always makes time for everyone."

moved to fill the gap which fulfilled the five spots. I know of no other man who could so easily have done this to the standard that was necessary and expected of those players.

A wonderfully talented player with both left and right feet and, of course, one of the finest headers of a ball - something lacking amongst many footballers of today.

The "Preston Plumber" with his late wife Elsie and children Brian and Barbara are all part of the Tom Finney legend.

After Tom's retirement from football and a gap of a few years, in 1971 he was invited to become President of that wonderful Deepdale Club, Preston North End. At that time the Club had little funding and the Chairman keeping the Club going was Alan Jones, a local businessman. Every Saturday morning a group of the directors who formed the Development Committee met to come up with ideas for raising funds to help the Club's finances. I was a member of that Committee. We had lots of fun and Tom, along with the directors of the day - Cyril Pilkington, Tom Gore, Jimmy Wilde, Michael Johnson, Gerald Brown - were many of the names that tried to keep the Club afloat.

These are the parts of Tom Finney the world has not seen - giving one of the most valuable commodities he had - his time - which was given freely by him week after week. Nearly every charity event would see Tom making himself available to help.

I have never known a person so talented who would be so attentive and pleasing. Tom is always willing to chat to anyone whatever part of society they might be from. He always makes time for everyone.

The highlight of acknowledgement came when the wishes of the fans of Preston were heard and Tom became Sir Tom Finney. After a long career of entertaining hundreds of thousands of fans for both his club and his country that is what a knighthood should be for and when it was given to him I felt it was one of the few times in today's world when you could say it was truly deserved.

Life with Tom at dinners and charity events was always eventful. I remember being at a Miss Great Britain event in Morecambe with Tom and Elsie. Elsie, sitting opposite me, put a glass down on an uneven table and it was not long before the glass of red wine was down the front of my shirt. Elsie apologised profusely. Having dried myself down Elsie returned with another glass and within minutes put it down on the uneven table and the same thing happened again. Tom looked across at me and said 'See, I always said she was dangerous!' That was just one of the many nice times I remember being with remarkable company.

Another story was when Tom heard that Palermo were interested in him. Tom was sent for by the chairman, Mr Taylor. He said *'Tom, Palermo are*

Top: Preston North End FC 1951
Above: Sir Tom arrives in Italy in 1952 with the England squad, but Palermo failed to lure him back with their £10,000 offer.
Opposite: Sir Tom and I in conversation at Deepdale

interested in you - go home and discuss it with Elsie and see me on Monday'. Tom went home and discussed it with Elsie and went back to see Mr Taylor on Monday. Tom knocked on the door and walked along the Long Room and stood before the Chairman.

'Mr Chairman,' said Tom.
'Before you say any more Tom,' said Mr Taylor, *'can you speak Italian?'*
'No, Mr Chairman' replied Tom.
'Well the job will be no good to you, Tom,' said Mr Taylor. *'I will have to tell them 'no'.'*

And that is just a small insight of the great man.

TREVOR J. HEMMINGS

PROUD TO SUPPORT SIR TOM'S CHARITIES

"We strive to support great causes and this is why we are honoured to support Sir Tom Finney Day and his chosen charities"...

Gareth Lewis, Barclays Community Relations Manager for the North West

Barclays has a long tradition of community and charity involvement going back to our Quaker roots. Ideas about community involvement have changed a lot since then. As a responsible bank, it is vital to us that we invest in the communities where we operate and ensure that our funding makes a positive impact. Our community work is based on partnership; we offer expertise and staff time, as well as financial investment, while our partners provide specialised knowledge and expertise.

We are proud to have one of the most developed corporate programmes in the UK with 1% of UK profits going into our community programme. Our total support during 2007 was £52.4 million.

We also strive to support great causes and this is why we are honoured to support Sir Tom Finney Day and his two chosen charities, CRY (Cardiac Risk in the Young) and The Baby Beat Appeal (Sharoe Green Maternity Unit, Royal Preston Hospital), both of which are invaluable in the local community.

I am sure that you will all join me in celebrating the fantastic achievements of Sir Tom Finney.

GARETH LEWIS
BARCLAYS COMMUNITY RELATIONS
MANAGER FOR THE NORTH WEST

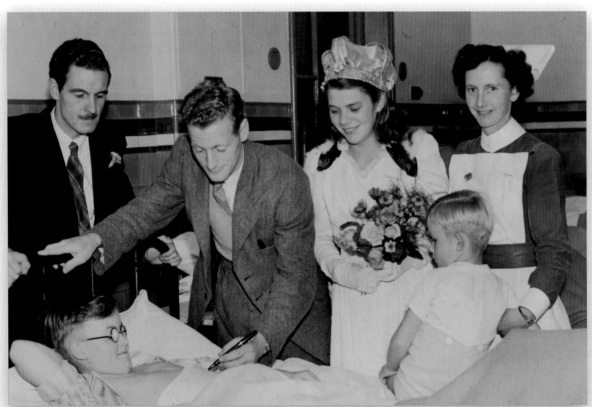

Tom takes time-out of his busy schedule to visit the children in the local hospital 1947

TO A SPECIAL MAN

"Sir Tom was one of the greatest footballers of the 20th century. He was one of only a small number of players who made his England debut before he made a full League debut for his Club."

Brian Barwick, Chief Executive, the FA

Tom Finney talks tactics after training with manager Cliff Britton, 1957

Tom had a particularly memorable match against Italy in Turin, scoring twice in England's 4-0 victory. The Italians were so impressed by Tom's display that one of their top sides tried to sign him. But he turned down their offer to stay with his beloved Preston North End.

Tom could play on either wing or at centre-forward. He was quick and he had an explosive shot. When he passed the ball, he could land it on a six pence. Remember those? He was the most sporting player too, never booked or sent off in his long career. Bill Shankly famously said that Tom could beat his marker if he was wearing an overcoat.

In the early 1980s, Bob Wilson and I interviewed Tom for a 'Football Focus Christmas Special.' After a very convivial chat we tied the four cans of film onto the roof of our car and started our journey back to London. On arrival we were mortified to find

those cans were missing. They were discovered by a member of the public in the road just outside Preston, who fortunately spotted Tom's name on them and took them to the local police station.

With Tom's help we were soon reunited with those cans and the interview was subsequently broadcast. Tom's modesty shone through and it all made for great television. Tom was a special footballer and remains a special man.

BRIAN BARWICK,
CHIEF EXECUTIVE, THE FA

Wembley '54

Captain Tom Finney proudly leads out his team to face
West Bromwich Albion in the 1954 FA Cup Final

NORTH END CUP FI

SEASON 1953-54 SOUVENIR, 1954 P

AUTOGRAPHS

FOOTBALL ASSOCIATION CHALLENGE CUP · SEASON 1953-54

DINNER AND DANCE

OF THE

PRESTON NORTH END
FOOTBALL CLUB

FINAL TIE
PRESTON NORTH END
VERSUS
WEST BROMWICH
ALBION

SAVOY HOTEL, LONDON, W.C.1 · MAY 1st, 1954

The Football Association Challenge Cup Final

**THE DIRECTORS OF THE
PRESTON NORTH END FOOTBALL CLUB LTD.**
request the pleasure of the company of

Mr. R. Holmes

at a Dinner and D
Savoy Hot

G. THOMPSON
W. CUNNINGHAM
J. WALTON
J. DOCHERTY
J. MARSTON

TOM FINNEY
Preston North End's International Outside Right and Captain.
"THE FOOTBALLER OF THE YEAR."

W. FORBES
R. FOSTER
C. WAYMAN
J. BAXTER
A. MORRISON

ONE OF THE TRUE GREATS!

"I sometimes ask myself, has there ever been a footballer more synonymous with a club than Sir Tom Finney is with Preston North End? And the answer is surely no!"

Chris Melia, Managing Director
C&M Construction Management Ltd

Finney in the dressing room after a hard game against Chelsea in 1960

Sir Tom spent his entire footballing career with Preston North End, his home town club, but the association runs far deeper than that. Sir Tom has lived in the town all his life, and I believe Sir Tom Finney, the man, has earned all the respect through a lifetime of dignity and loyalty. Fundamentally, however, all the recognition he has received is due to his overwhelming brilliance as a footballer. Having not seen Sir Tom play myself I have spoken to former players and people who have been involved in the world of sport, and the overwhelming consensus from his peers is that he is one of the true greats!

Although there is a tendency to treat with scepticism the claims to greatness of players like Sir Tom from a certain era, the fact is that Sir Tom has not been done any favours by the lack of television footage of him in action compared to other players of latter day. There can be no doubting his majesty on a football field.

Indeed, among his contemporaries Sir Tom Finney's claims to being considered as one of the greatest of them all remain strongly championed and the statistics uphold Sir Tom's greatness!

I would personally like to pay tribute to what Sir Tom has given to the world of football, and express how you would struggle to find any comparison to his commitment, passion and greatness in the modern game.

CHRIS MELIA,
MANAGING DIRECTOR,
C&M CONSTRUCTION
MANAGEMENT LTD

THE GREAT ALL-ROUNDER

*"As well as being the football hero to lads of my generation,
Sir Tom excelled in many other ways."*

Malcolm Rae OBE

*One of Sir Tom's great friends and cricketing hero,
Yorkshire and England's fast bowler Freddie Trueman, fondly known as 'Fiery Fred'*

Tom was an all-round cricketer, a steady right handed batsman and described as a decent slow left arm bowler. In fact one of Sir Tom's great friends and cricketing hero was Yorkshire and England's fast bowler Freddie Trueman, fondly known as 'Fiery Fred'!

My friend Fred Wilson recalled playing in the annual fixture, PNE versus Fulwood and Broughton CC. He overheard PNE's captain for the day, Eddie Quigley, asking Tom to open, to which Tom replied "do you mean the door!" This reveals Tom's endearing humour and modesty.

Apparently early on in the game Fred appealed for a plumb LBW, to which the umpire responded, pointing to the crowd, "They have come to see him not you!" When he eventually got Tom out, stumped, Fred was widely booed!

Sir Tom further achieved the respect and regard of the people of Preston for his citizenship and services to the community as a magistrate, and chairman of the local health authority.
At the time of his appointment, rumour had it that the Secretary of State, Norman Fowler, asked Ken Clarke who should be the next Chair in Preston. Ken Clarke replied, "there used to be a good right winger in Preston called Finney!"

I am delighted to be given the opportunity to salute the life and career of Sir Tom; he is a jewel of a man.

MALCOLM RAE OBE

THE MASTER OF ALL CONDITIONS

"Having had my transfer request granted at Aston Villa, I had a number of clubs interested in buying me, but when I found out that Preston North End were one of them my mind was made up for me. Besides being nearer to 'home', they had the legendary Tom Finney playing for them on the right-wing."

Tommy 'Topper' Thompson

Being a goalscorer and having already played alongside Tom for England and the Football League I just knew that I would enjoy playing next to him, week in week out. We hit it off immediately, as we scored 14 goals between us in the first ten games we played together. Telepathy or not, we clicked, we could read each other's game. We did not practice moves in training in those days, training was more for fitness levels, but self-discipline was very important to us. During our second season together Tom was switched from the wing to the centre-forward position. He had another lease of life in this position and many great judges thought that he was the best centre-forward in the league. He found more freedom in the middle compared to the wings.

Tom Finney was a great player to feed off, he had amazing ability, especially for a 34-year-old plumber. He was strong legged, full of spring, good in the air, very talented, but also naturally gifted. Tom was a master of all conditions, in that he could perform on any surface. Some of those pitches we had to play on in those days compared to today's excellent 'carpets'... it makes you shudder to think back. In retrospect Tom was probably 'over used' by the Club, playing for the cause when not always fully fit. The trouble was he was a huge asset to the Club, putting thousands on the gate if he played.

I personally believe that Tom might have played on a bit longer if not for the manager, Cliff Britton, who at times had some strange ideas.

But we have some great memories playing together against, and beating, the best teams around. It was a good era to be a spectator too, as scores such as 8-0 vs Birmingham, 7-1 vs Portsmouth, 6-1 vs Manchester City and 4-5 vs Chelsea will testify.

Tom was world class, that's the way to describe him. You have to earn Footballer of the Year awards and he did that twice! It was an honour to be associated with him both on and off the pitch.

TOMMY THOMPSON

During their first three seasons (1955 to 1958) Tom Finney and Tommy Thompson played together for Preston North End a total of 104 games, scoring an amazing 145 goals between them... a phenomenal partnership you must agree.
(Ian Rigby, PNE historian)

CELEBRATING AN EXCEPTIONAL MAN

"The League Managers Association is delighted to be able to pay tribute to an outstanding footballer and a true gentleman, revered in the world of football both for his skills as a player and his genuine passion for the sport."

Sir Tom inspired many fans and young players during his early years at Preston North End, but has since gained the respect of many more people involved in football. In particular, several of our members, having managed Preston during their career, were fortunate enough to benefit from his positive outlook and significant insight into the club, its players and the sport itself.

Sir Tom Finney is an ambassador for the sport in the true sense of the word and on behalf of all our members, the LMA is proud to be able to celebrate an exceptional man and we are delighted to have been invited to be part of the first 'Sir Tom Finney Day'.

Howard Wilkinson,
LMA Chairman

"I am delighted to have the opportunity to pay tribute to Sir Tom Finney. He is remembered around the world as one of the greatest players in England's history. I am told that at one time, after helping England to beat Italy 4-0 in Turin, Sir Tom was offered the chance to play club football in Italy with Palermo. He chose to stay with his hometown club in Preston and I am sure that was a loss to Italian football but a big gain for supporters in Preston and England."
Fabio Capello,
LMA President and Manager, England

"My first experience of Sir Tom Finney is not one of joy.... as I stood in the terraces of Hampden Park and watched him giving one of my heroes in the Scotland Team, Sammy Cox, a roasting. Winding forward all these years and actually meeting the man restores any lost faith you may have in humanity as he is such a wonderful person and so humble. Why can't we all be like that? A credit to the town of Preston, his Football Club and his family, well done Sir Tom."
Sir Alex Ferguson CBE,
LMA Committee Member
and Manager, Manchester United

"As a player, he was a manager's dream. For England, he played left wing, right wing and centre forward. He was even wanted by a top Italian club but the Chairman said he was not going. Tom said thank you and went off on holiday. Imagine that these days? I am delighted to pay tribute to such a wonderful man."
Lawrie McMenemy MBE,
LMA Vice President

"Tom, you made fans of all of us who were privileged to see you play, thank you for that."
Dave Bassett,
LMA Committee Member

"A boyhood hero of many, a player of wonderful balance and great skill, but as importantly a loyal club man who was both brilliant yet humble."
David Pleat, LMA Committee Member

"Sir Tom Finney - it's been my pleasure to know Tom for many years. I was fortunate to work with him at Preston North End as both player and coach whilst he was President at the club. Not only was he a great player and ambassador for Preston but a gentleman in every sense of the word."
Sam Allardyce,
LMA Committee Member

"A great player and a real gentleman."
Frank Clark,
LMA Vice Chairman

"My admiration and respect for such a gentleman and true professional grew enormously when I had the privilege of working with Sir Tom at PNE. I wonder, how much would a 'Tom Finney' be worth in today's transfer market?"
Billy Davies,
former Manager,
Preston North End
(2004 to 2006)

"He was justifiably honoured by Her Majesty and affectionately known to everyone as 'Sir Tom'. That Sir Tom is regarded with respect and great affection is not surprising. To me, and all Preston North End managers, he was consistently supportive, never voicing criticism."
Craig Brown,
former Manager,
Preston North End
(2002 to 2004)

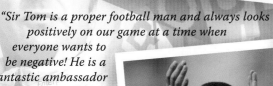

"Sir Tom is a proper football man and always looks positively on our game at a time when everyone wants to be negative! He is a fantastic ambassador to the game of football and Preston North End, through all his hours of charity work."
Paul Simpson,
Manager, Shrewsbury Town and former Manager, Preston North End (2006 to 2007)

"Sir Tom was a great help to me in the early stages of my management career. He has an incredible passion for the game and he is somebody I have got great admiration for. There is no doubt he was one of the greatest players, but to me, he is also a great man."
David Moyes,
Manager, Everton and former Manager, Preston North End (1998 to 2002)

Jimmy Armfield   Nat Lofthouse   Alex Parker   Bert Trautm

Stan Matthews   Stan Mortenson

PERHAPS THE GREATEST TEAM TO PLAY AT DEEPDALE?

Wilf Mannion   **Billy Liddell**   **Bill Shankly**

...nney   **Neil Franklin**   **Billy Wright**

Above signatures from every
member of the allstar invitational team.

Sir Tom Finney Testimonial 1960
Sir Tom Finney reminisces with members of an allstar invitational team at his testimonial game in 1960

THE PRESTON PLUMBER AND THE BUILDERS FROM LONGRIDGE

"We welcome the opportunity to pay tribute to Sir Tom Finney, an aristocrat on the football field and a true gentleman and shrewd businessman off the field."

Walter Carefoot & Sons (Construction) Ltd

On the stage at Longridge

The lasting tribute

The work begins in May

We look back with fondness not only to the pleasure Sir Tom has given us with his football mastery but also to the many charitable fund raising events he has supported over the years. Pictured is a young Tom Finney and Walter Carefoot at a fundraising event for local football club Longridge Celtic in 1952.

Our association has continued as contractors for many years and 'The Preston Plumber' and the 'builders from Longridge' have completed many fine projects together up until and beyond Sir Tom's retirement. It was also an honour to be associated with the lasting tribute to Sir Tom when PNE appointed Carefoots as principle contractor to carry out the works involved in recreating the 'Splash' statue in May 2006.

Sir Tom earning another 'cap'

WALTER CAREFOOT & SONS (CONSTRUCTION) LTD
Blackpool Road, Longridge nr Preston PR2 3NR
Tel: 01772 783711

1 Froghall Lane, Warrington, Cheshire WA2 7JJ
Tel: 01925 259136
www.carefootplc.com

CAREFOOT PLC

TOP DRAW

"It is both an honour and privilege to pay tribute to Sir Tom Finney, a football legend and a true gentleman who is undoubtedly one of the greatest footballers the world has ever seen."

Ian Penrose CEO, The New Football Pools
Proud Sponsor of Sir Tom Finney Exhibition and Gala Night - March 2009

Having been born and brought up in Preston and being an ardent supporter of North End since a young boy, some of my earliest footballing memories are centred around Sir Tom. In the mid 1970's, when it was not uncommon to turn up at Deepdale a couple of minutes before kick-off, my brothers and I would regularly listen to our father telling us how years ago he used to arrive no later than 1.30pm to secure his place on the Spion Kop to watch 'The Preston Plumber' displaying his mesmerising skills.

My father impressed on me what an incredibly versatile player Sir Tom was, playing in all the orthodox five forward positions for the Lilywhites (his one and only club), and appearing for England at right-wing, left-wing and centre-forward. He really had it all – speed, balance, pinpoint passing and for a man of no great height, could head with awesome power.

"The Pools Panel was something new, but talking about football was the next best thing to playing, so I took to it like a duck to water"

Sir Tom Finney

It was shortly after his retirement that Sir Tom began his long association with the Football Pools. The winter of 1962/63 was one of the worst Britain had ever experienced. From Boxing Day 1962 until the middle of March 1963, it was as if someone had thrown a giant white blanket over every street, field, river and football ground. Football matches were postponed, sometimes for weeks on end.

During this period of near Siberian weather, the Football Pools Panel was born. They would determine the results of games that were postponed or cancelled. It felt only natural that Sir Tom should be one of the original members of the Football Pools Panel which first met in London on 26 January 1963.

Of course, since then football has undergone a sea change and so has the Football Pools. Now re-launched as The New Football Pools and offering a range of online football games, you can rest assured that we will, together with our charitable contributions to football, sport and the arts, which have exceeded £1.1 billion, continue to play a role in the development of football in the UK at all levels.

Would football be where it is today without the past influence of the superstars of yesteryear, players of the calibre and character of Sir Tom Finney? I, for one, very much doubt it.

IAN PENROSE,
CEO, THE NEW FOOTBALL POOLS

TOM FINNEY   TOMMY LAWTON

The Chairman of the Pools Selection Board, Lord Brabazon, shares a joke with fellow board members Tom Finney, Tommy Lawton and George Young as they predict results for the weekend matches cancelled due to the 'Big Freeze' 26th January 1963.

The New Football Pools

LUCK OF THE IRISH

Tom Finney comes out of retirement 25th September 1963

After much deliberation, Tom Finney, then aged 41, was persuaded to come out of retirement by the Distillery manager, Mr George Eastham, for a one-off game to be played at Windsor Park, Belfast. It was the first round of the 1963/64 European Cup competition. Tom had been officially registered for the game since 15th August when Mr Eastham had crossed the Irish Sea to meet up with Tom at his business office in Moor Lane, Preston. Tom, who had been in training with the Preston North End juniors one night a week, solely to keep fit for the numerous benefit and testimonial games he was invited to play in, stepped up his training programme to make sure he did not let the Irish team, or himself down.

On leaving Speke airport Tom said: "I am looking forward to the match immensely. I accepted with reluctance, but having done so, for this one match only, I will do by best". Windsor Park had been a lucky ground for Tom in the past, he had made his England debut there in 1946, and scored, and his 30th and final goal for England was also scored there, in 1958. It was certainly a night for Tom Finney to turn back the clock. He met up with his new teammates on the day of the game and was selected to play centre-forward and was made captain the side.

A Belfast Correspondence relayed the following information:-

"Tom Finney is the cause of both jubilation and regret amongst Northern Ireland fans today. The jubilation stems from the contribution the former Preston North End and England star made last night at Windsor Park, Belfast in the astonishing 3-3 draw made against the Portuguese champions, Benfica. The regret was because Tom will not be going to Lisbon next week with the part-timers from Distillery for the second leg of the tie.

"It took less than one minute for the Irish to score. It was Finney's high leap, which enabled him to head the ball, throwing the Benfica defence into disarray, allowing wing-half Kennedy to score. Benfica's experience helped draw them level, but then on 25 minutes Finney shared in the moved that lead to left-winger Hamilton regaining the lead for his side, a lead they held until the hour mark. Benfica then hit the Irish with a quick one-two, scoring twice in two minutes, the first of those goals being scored by Eusebio. Then a Finney-inspired Distillery eventually equalised ten minutes from time and held on for a very respectable draw against top class opposition."

It was difficult to believe that 41-year-old Finney had not played league football for three seasons, he had made a mockery of his years.

Finney praised his team-mates for their courage and for not suffering an inferior complex against a great European team, and said "I got a real kick out of helping this wonderful Distillery team to draw against one of the world's best teams and I wish them well in the second leg."

SIR TOM FINNEY
THE PRIDE OF KENDAL TOWN

Photograph: courtesy of The Westmorland Gazette

Congratulations to Sir Tom from all the committee management,
players and supporters of Kendal Town on his big day.
The Club are very proud and privileged to have Sir Tom as their club president!

MR PRESTON NORTH END

I first met Sir Tom 19 years ago when I became sponsor of the Preston North End shirts in the 1990/91 season. Part of my involvement with the Club back then meant access to the boardroom and I met Sir Tom during that period of time. It was quite clear to me, from hearing about a legend, just why the man has become a legend.

Sir Tom is a man who has so much time for anybody. He still received more mail than anybody at the Football Club. He always has a gathering around his car parking space about an hour before every home game, because supporters know he will be arriving with his son, Brian.

He signs all the autographs carefully, in nice neat handwriting – a little bit more thought goes into it than today's modern professionals, but that is what the man is all about.

I never saw Sir Tom play, but I heard plenty about him from my father. Strangely enough, when I was a lad, it wasn't what you always wanted to hear because Preston North End were struggling in the lower reaches and all the older generation would just talk about 'the great PNE sides and how we missed Tom Finney'.

When we opened our fourth stand we entertained Crystal Palace and introduced a number of legends to the crowd at half-time. At the end of introductions of the other players the 'main' legend's name was announced and, to a man, all the visiting supporters from Crystal Palace stood up and joined our own fans to welcome Sir Tom onto the pitch and that is what this man is about to English football.

It is proud to be associated with a Club where such a great and honourable man is the President. He is not just Mr Preston North End, he is Mr Preston and it is fantastic that I have been given this opportunity to be able to speak about someone I and everyone connected with Preston North End are so proud to know.

DEREK SHAW, CHAIRMAN
PRESTON NORTH END FOOTBALL CLUB

I only met Sir Tom Finney once or twice before becoming the manager at Preston North End, when I visited Deepdale to watch games with David Moyes. Therefore, everything thing I knew about him then was what the vast majority of people knew, about what a fantastic player he was and what a great career he had.

Since I joined the Club I have found out what a terrific man he is as well. It is wonderful to be in his company and I tell my dad about it all the time, because he is a massive fan of Sir Tom's and he is always thrilled that I have been in his company, as am I.

Although Sir Tom was playing before I was watching, his reputation goes before him and what he has achieved is amazing. My favourite players were always wingers and, being a winger myself, my dad would always talk to me about the best wingers of the time, namely Sir Tom and Sir Stanley Matthews. Coincidentally I met Sir Stanley Matthews up at Hampden Park when he came up to visit and it was a big thrill to meet him, as it is a big thrill to meet Sir Tom. I find him very interesting and terrific company.

He is a legendary figure in Preston, and rightly so. He is held in great esteem not only for his playing career and everything he achieved in the game, but also for the fact that he is such a nice man and is so generous with his time. The number of events I go to and Sir Tom is there is incredible. He obviously still has a great deal of time and passion for football and life in general and I think it is amazing that he gives back as much as he does to people.

I am sure he was a model professional. Like all the great players he is humble and that is a great quality for someone to have. He does not see what he did as something special, but everyone else knows it was. Whenever I have spoken to really great players that is how they tend to come over and Sir Tom is certainly one of them.

ALAN IRVINE, MANAGER
PRESTON NORTH END FOOTBALL CLUB

Alan Irvine and Sir Tom Finney take a look at their new signing for Preston North End

Paper Innovation Ltd are extremely proud to be associated with Preston North End FC and the PNE Former Players Association. We would like to take this opportunity to congratulate Sir Tom Finney on an outstanding career and his dedication to so many worthwhile causes. From all at Paper Innovation, Steve Johnston, Wendy, Hayley, Anna-Louise, Blake and Brett.

more than meets the eye   **t** 01772 562 526 | www. paperinnovation .co.u

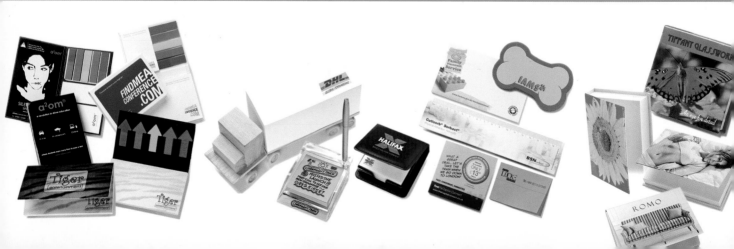

THE PHANTOM WINGER

"As a young fan on the terraces at Preston North End, I have heard countless stories of the club's glory years. The overwhelming majority featured the one man: The Phantom Winger - Sir Tom Finney."

Steve Johnston, Managing Director, Paper Innovation Ltd

I met Sir Tom at a function 11 years ago. It was a great honour for my company, Paper Innovation, to be asked to sponsor the event. Following the success of this evening, the Preston North End Former Players Association was inaugurated. Sir Tom was appointed as the president and Paper Innovation were proud to be one of the initial sponsors. Our association with PNE Former Players has been most worthwhile and I very much enjoyed getting to know the players I have heard so much about over the years, none more so than Sir Tom.

For a footballer held in such high esteem, Sir Tom is implausibly down to earth. Modest and humble, he finds time and consideration for everyone he meets. He has shown dedication and support for many charity efforts as well, of course, for his beloved Preston North End.

His energy and enthusiasm for football and socialising continue uncompromisingly, as does his quick wit and wry sense of humour. I look forward to telling my sons about the Preston North End and England legend who sat them on his knee and joined in their laughter.

Thank you for the memories on and off the pitch Sir Tom.

STEVE JOHNSTON, MANAGING DIRECTOR
PAPER INNOVATION LTD

The anecdotes range from the incredible to the unbelievable. Sir Tom was a natural in any position on the pitch and with either foot. I've even heard that he once jumped above the crossbar and headed down into the net.

Those who have seen him play describe his performances as mesmerising, his talent immense. He took command of the field and bewildered entire defences single-handedly.

For many years, I had wished that I could have been on the terraces during the period that an England legend graced the Deepdale turf and experienced the magic for myself.

Forty years - of the glory and heartache that following Preston North End brings - later, I have not seen any player at Deepdale to compare to Sir Tom and fill this void. However, I can proudly say that knowing Tom Finney the man has almost compensated for never having seen Tom Finney the player.

THE ALL-TIME GREAT OF BRITISH FOOTBALL

"The word 'great' is much over used in football today for players of modest ability and questionable moral standards. Sir Tom Finney is, however, someone who can truly be labelled with this word."

Lawrence Gosling, Football Monthly Archives

As a player he was described as the finest he had ever seen by the legendary Bill Shankly, which in itself was no hollow accolade. Shankly had the rare benefit of playing with or seeing many of the greatest players of the first 70 years of the last century - and rarely is a Scotsman so complimentary about an Englishman! But Sir Tom was not only a fine player; he is also a fine man. His humility, modesty and dedication to one club and one town are what contributed to him being rightly described as an all-time great of British football. He has retained that from the moment he hung up his boots to today.

The heyday of Sir Tom's career in many ways mirrors the golden days of Charles Buchan's Football Monthly, launched in September 1951, and, some might argue the golden days of British football. His appearance in many issues of the magazine were testament to both his popularity and dedication to the game, such as in the November 1951 issue when Sir Tom wrote an article explaining how to trap the ball, which no doubt inspired budding footballers the length and breadth of the United Kingdom.

Sir Tom has outlasted the magazine in its original format by three decades and we are honoured to be associated with this annual celebration of his life.

LAWRENCE GOSLING,
CHARLES BUCHAN'S
FOOTBALL MONTHLY ARCHIVES

Charles Buchan's Football Monthly is now available electronically in PDF format. The archives are currently used as content on football websites and by publishers, educationalists, film producers and gift designers. In conjunction with English Heritage and Malavan Media, a range of gift books using original articles and information from the magazine has also been published. These include The Best of Charles Buchan's Football Monthly, The Best of Manchester United, The Best of Arsenal, The Best of Liverpool and The Best of Spurs. Further information can be found at **www.footballmonthlyarchives.co.uk**.

All images and content of Charles Buchan's Football Monthly copyright © Football Monthly Limited

Top: September 1954 issue featuring Tom and his son.
Above: A photo of Tom and his son from the same time.
Right: A selection of front covers featuring legends of the game.

CHARLES BUCHAN'S FOOTBALL MONTHLY

1/6

by
UCHAN

THOMPSON

Articles by
RAY
LANE
LEWIN
AMSEY

ge Pictures
TAYLOR
ALLCHURCH
McILROY
NY CAREY
MEDLEY
E ROBLEDO
CHARLES
HANCOCKS
UR WRIGHT

Charles Buchan's FOOTBALL MONTHLY

1/6
Overseas Price 2'-
Forces Overseas 1'6
MARCH 1958

DUNCAN EDWARDS
Manchester United and England

BERT TRAUTMANN
Manchester City

1/6
Overseas Price 2/-
Forces Overseas 1/6
DECEMBER 1958

FOOTBALL MONTHLY
APRIL 1953

Inside :
MY STORY BY
ESSE PYE
ll-Colour
ure of
Froggatt

Charles Buchan's FOOTBALL MONTHLY

APRIL 1955 1/6
Overseas Price 2/-
Forces Overseas 1 6

CHARLES BUCHAN'S FOOTBALL
MAY, 1954

OOTBALL MONTH

JIMMY GREAVES
Chelsea and England

The World's Greatest Soccer Magazine

TOMMY DOCHERTY
Preston North End and Scotland

CHARLES Buchan's FOOTBALL MONTHLY

1/6

SEPTEMBER 1951

The Magazine of Britain's National Game

Edited by
CHARLES BUCHAN
and
JOHN THOMPSON

Cover Picture
STANLEY MATTHEWS
Blackpool & England

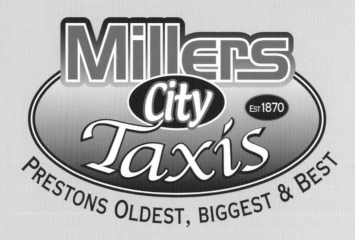

PRESTON'S MOST FAMOUS SON

"Sir Tom Finney is Preston through and through and the whole city is rightly proud of our 'most famous son'."

Councillor John Swindells, Mayor of Preston

Sir Tom is known all over the world for his football achievements mesmerising fans with his glorious skills in both feet. Sir Tom famously played the whole of his career for Preston North End which is testament to him, the Football Club and Preston as a whole.

As an England international Sir Tom catapulted Preston and Preston North End on to the international stage, and he remains one of England's all time leading goalscorers - not bad for a plumber from Preston.

As a football icon, young players from across the world could not have a better role model. Someone with great skill but also great dignity and sense of fair play. Indeed another football legend and former PNE player Bill Shankly said of Sir Tom: "He would have been great in any team, in any match and in any age - even if he had been wearing an overcoat."

It takes a very special person to transcend the boundaries of football and become a national treasure, but Sir Tom is a wonderful and unassuming man. He has done so much for his home town that words do not really do him enough justice.

Even now at 86 Sir Tom is president of Preston North End, a role which he fulfils with the grace and dignity befitting a knight of the realm.

As a modest man, Sir Tom makes light of his contribution to charity work and civic life. That's why everyone loves Sir Tom and he puts a smile on the face of everyone he meets - young and old alike.

He really is 'Mr Preston' and the best possible ambassador for the city. As a freeman of Preston, Sir Tom already has the highest possible honour that the City can bestow on him but through the Sir Tom Finney Day there is an opportunity for the whole community to celebrate with Sir Tom and mark his unique contribution to the City and the people of Preston.

COUNCILLOR JOHN SWINDELLS
MAYOR OF PRESTON

SilverDell
Home-made Ice Cream

THE PERFECT PROFESSIONAL FOOTBALLER

"Unfortunately I never got see Tom play for Preston or England but not only is he admired throughout England and the world as one of the greatest footballers to ever grace a pitch, he is equally respected in this area for the undying work he has carried for Preston North End Football Club."

Richard Ormishaw,
Managing Director, Kingsley Asset Finance Limited

In these days of spiraling players' wages where, every week seems to unveil a new tabloid scandal about a top-flight player, it is fantastic that Sir Tom is remembered with such great affection for his marvellous football skills and his efforts on behalf of Preston North End Football Club.

Although Preston didn't win a major honour, during his career, Tom's total mastery of all the required footballing techniques triumphed over the lack of medals. His versatility, allowing him to play in all the orthodox five forward positions of the day for Preston and appearing for England at right-wing, left-wing and centre-forward, was astounding. A feat that will surely never be repeated in the modern game of one footed players. But his amazing heading ability in addition to his other skills made him truly unique. Think of his earning power if he was a player in this day and age.

Only Matt le Tissier in the modern era has matched Tom's dedication to one team and it is to his eternal credit that Tom stuck with Preston despite the lure of the Italian lira.

Kingsley Finance Limited is delighted to be associated with this tribute to Sir Tom and we continue our huge support of Tom and his continuing efforts to help the club and people of Preston.

RICHARD ORMISHER
KINGSLEY ASSET FINANCE LIMITED

Kingsley
FINANCE LIMITED

Left: Even the weather will not stop Tom from playing! Tom is pictured brushing the Deepdale pitch.
Right: A 1940's cigarette card.

FINNEY FOR ENGLAND

Northern Ireland's Windsor Park was the venue in September 1946, not only for England's first post-war international, but also the debut of one of England's finest ever players, Tom Finney.

He partnered another legend, Raich Carter, on the right-wing, had a terrific debut and scored one of the goals in a 7-2 win. Two days later England moved south to Dublin and beat the Republic of Ireland 1-0. It was Finney who scored the late winner for his side.

Playing in the England team in the late 1940s gave Finney the chance to perform alongside some of the greatest players to have worn the white shirt. Frank Swift, Billy Wright, Carter, Tommy Lawton, George Hardwick and Wilf Mannion were just a few of the footballing legends turning out for their country at that time. It was also an age when goal chances were in abundance, and with Finney an expert, not only in making goals but also in scoring them, it was a good time to watch the national team.

Against Portugal in May 1947, Finney played on the left-wing to enable Stanley Matthews to come in at number seven. It was the first time the two players had been in the same England team and the 62,000 spectators then watched a master-class of wing play as Portugal were ripped apart. England won 10-0 and

Finney, amongst other things, scored a wonder goal. Picking the ball up on the halfway line he swerved past one defender after another and then beat the goalkeeper from the narrowest of angles. Then, in a 5-2 win over Belgium, Finney scored twice, and both goals were made by Matthews, who was in inspired form.

Amongst the older fans of Portugal there will always be a soft spot for the Preston Plumber, even though he saved some of his best performances when playing against their team. Finney scored six goals against Portugal and in May 1950, in Lisbon, he played at outside-right and scored four

times in a 5-3 win. His third goal followed a classic dribble and fierce shot, so typically Finney.

Finney then played in his first World Cup finals in 1950 when he travelled with the squad to Brazil. England beat Chile 2-0 in their first game, played in the Maracana Stadium in Rio de Janeiro. Finney played on the wing and was in good form, making the second goal with a run and cross to Wilf Mannion who

In Finney's 76 games for England the team lost just twelve times.

scored. The next group match though was probably the lowest point of Finney's England career. They lost a game against the USA, a humiliating 1-0 defeat that is still remembered to this day. Another 1-0 defeat against Spain in the final group game then put England out of the competition, although in that match Finney was twice sent sprawling in the penalty area with the referee turning a blind eye. After the competition Finney was the only England player to be voted into the world team selected from the participants.

Although often in sparkling form, Finney did have a few quiet games for his country, and indeed, he was occasionally accused of over-elaborating during possession. But then, to prove his talent beyond doubt, in May 1948 he had a memorable match in Turin against the powerful Italy side. This time at outside-left, he showed all his sublime skills, scoring twice in a stunning 4-0 win. It was Finney's 15th cap before he finally finished on the losing side for England and in his 76 games the team lost just twelve times. The worst of those defeats came in Budapest, against Hungary. Finney had missed the infamous 6-3 home defeat against the Magnificent Magyars in 1953, but there was no escape when the two teams met again six months later. England lost 7-1 and Finney had a game to forget, missing chances and seeing his team outclassed.

Tom Finney was certainly able to see the world when playing for England and he visited 21 countries during his international career. Of his 76 caps he only played 30 of them at home and just 16 games at Wembley. The perfect playing

surface of our national stadium did suit his dribbling and passing skills though. He had some excellent games there, although of course, he did have one of his poorest games when he played for Preston at Wembley, against WBA in the 1954 FA Cup Final.

Finney had a fine England record against Scotland, one reason why, to this day, the Scottish football fans still marvel when talking about the Preston player. He was especially effective at Hampden Park and never lost a game there in six appearances. In fact five of those games ended in an England victory

and Finney scored some amazing goals at Hampden, as well as memorably setting up a debut goal for the brilliant prodigy, Bobby Charlton. Finney's brilliant left-wing dribble and cross to the edge of the area was met by a Charlton volley that was past the keeper before he could move.

In 1958 Finney had another chance to impress at a World Cup finals, but the great player was really unlucky. After impressing against Russia in a 2-2 draw, scoring the late penalty past Lev Yashin which netted a draw, the Preston star was injured and, alas, did not feature in the other games. It was a disappointing end to his World Cup adventure.

Ironically it was Russia who were the opponents for his last England appearance in October 1958. The match was at Wembley and England won 5-0 with Finney having a relatively quiet game. In that match Tom's good friend Nat Lofthouse of Bolton, scored his 30th international goal, thus equalling Finney's record total.

Vme CHAMPIONNAT DU MONDE - COUPE JULES RIMET 1954

SUISSE

Légitimation - Ausweis

Joueur - Spieler

Nom: Finney

Prénoms: T.

Pays: England

F.I.F.A.
Le Secrétaire général

FINNEY MAGIC

The 1957/8 season was arguably the last great season enjoyed by Preston North End Football Club.

The Two Toms - Finney and Thompson during training at Deepdale

It saw some great attacking football, North End scoring 100 league goals, Tom Finney at his best in an awesome partnership with Tommy Thompson, and a runners-up spot, which could have been even better.

After a quiet start to the campaign, Preston, crucially as it turned out, lost four of their first six games. The prolific pairing of Finney and Thompson then found their rhythm and proceeded to rip first division defences apart. It so nearly gave the club its elusive third League Championship. It was a 3-1 win at White Hart Lane against Spurs that really ignited the season. Finney's link play that day in his roving centre-forward role had the home defenders chasing shadows. Thompson scored twice that day and in the next game, at home to Manchester City, everything came together with Finney giving a masterclass performance.

Superb ball control, delightful passing and two brilliant goals, the second and the sixth, tore City apart. Finney's first goal followed a devastating run down the left, a cut inside and a fine shot into the far corner, a brilliant example of close control and deadly finishing.

Although Finney wore the number nine shirt for most of this season, much of his finest work was done on the wings, either left or right. His was a roving role that dovetailed superbly with the talents of Thompson, Sammy Taylor, Derek Mayers and the mercurial Jimmy Baxter. It didn't always work however, and sometimes not everyone was quite tuned in as many brilliant pieces of Finney skill proved profitless through the faltering of others.

As the season progressed, opposition managers realised that to stop Preston they had to stop Finney. Easier said than done! At Newcastle, for instance, tough tackling Bob Stokoe was even booed by his own fans for his unceremonious treatment of the peerless Preston Plumber.

Finney's goalscoring record included many penalty kicks, often after he himself had been fouled. He scored five during this campaign, some placed, some struck hard and true, but even Finney was not averse to missing a penalty. Against Leicester at Deepdale in March 1958, he missed two in one match! One shot struck a post and the other was a weak effort easily saved. Preston won the game 4-1, but the annoying thing was that Finney would have

The nickname "The Magnet", which was often attributed to Finney, was never more evident than during this season.

completed an elusive hat-trick for Preston that day had he scored them both. He never did achieve that feat in his career with the Club.

The nickname "The Magnet", which was often attributed to Finney, was never more evident than during this season. As he roved, two, three and sometimes even four defenders went with him. As often as not though, Finney would still get the better of his markers. His adept passing skills took defenders out of the game and regularly set up chances for his colleagues, emphasised by a record 100 league goals scored that year.

It was noticeable how many times Finney's shots on goal were low and hard, aimed at the corners. Many goals came like that, as against Everton at Deepdale. A pass by Joe Walton sent Finney away down the left. A quick shuffle and side-step took him past a bewildered defender and Finney then homed

OFFICIAL PROGRAMME 4ᴰ

EVERTON FOOTBALL CLUB

GOODISON PARK. LIVERPOOL

FOOTBALL LEAGUE DIVISION ONE

Nottingham Forest FOOTBALL CLUB City Ground, Nottingham

Nottm. Forest v. Preston North End
Saturday, August 24th, 1957

PRESTON NORTH END v. BLACKBURN ROVERS
at Deepdale, Easter Monday, April 10th, 1950

THE MAGNET.—Finney draws Eckersley, Horton and Holt

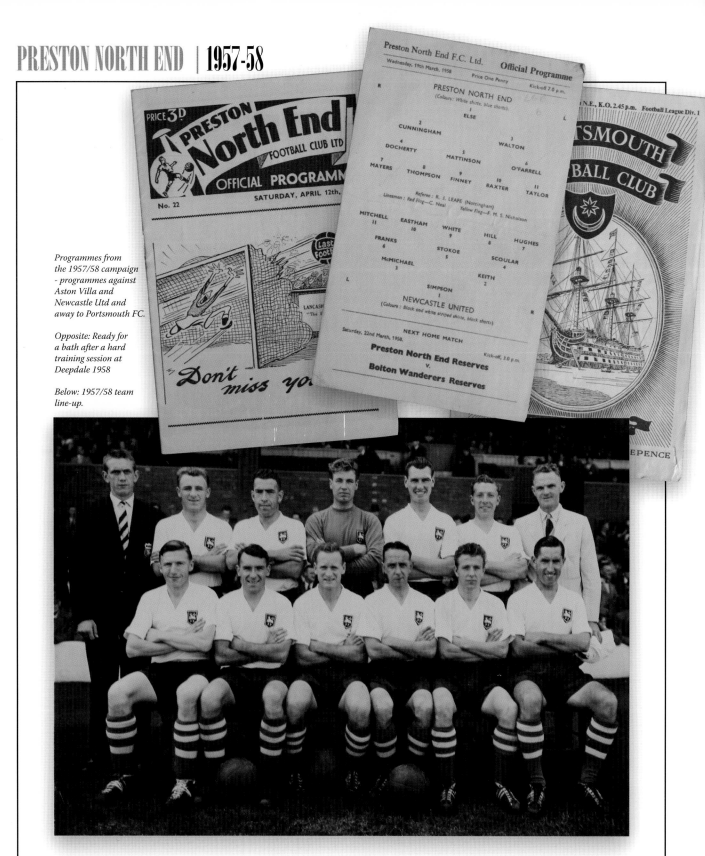

Programmes from the 1957/58 campaign - programmes against Aston Villa and Newcastle Utd and away to Portsmouth FC.

Opposite: Ready for a bath after a hard training session at Deepdale 1958

Below: 1957/58 team line-up.

in on goal. A perfectly timed and well-executed right foot shot low into the far corner sent Preston on the way to another victory.

Two things are often forgotten when analysing Finney's play; one was his power in the air, and the other was his ability to perform all his skills on some very poor playing surfaces. Today's top stars enjoy the luxury of performing week in, week out on pitches that look like carpets. But back then, even Deepdale was poor at times. The big heavy balls, the cloying mud and the bruising defenders all took

their toll, but Finney always rose above all of that and just got on with it. As far as his heading ability goes, his incredibly strong thigh muscles enabled him to outjump many defenders much taller than himself, but more than that he had the knack of being able to head down, and accurately.

Finney's talents were never better seen than in 1957/58, what a shame that North End were pipped to the title by the brilliant Wolves side led by England captain Billy Wright. It deprived Finney the one prize he craved for, a League Championship medal.

Above left and above: Finney addresses an emotional crowd surrounded by players and officials as he says goodbye to Deepdale.
Left: Finney beats his marker during his last game against Luton Town.
Below: Preston players sing Auld Lang Syne before Finney's last game.

Top: Another angle showing a
surrounded Finney addressing the crowd.
Top right: Finney centres the ball watched by a Luton defender.
Middle: Well wishers congratulate Finney on his retirement as he
prepares to lead his team out on to the pitch one last time.
Middle right: Finney swings in
another pin-point corner watched
by thousands of adoring fans.
Below: The match day programme.

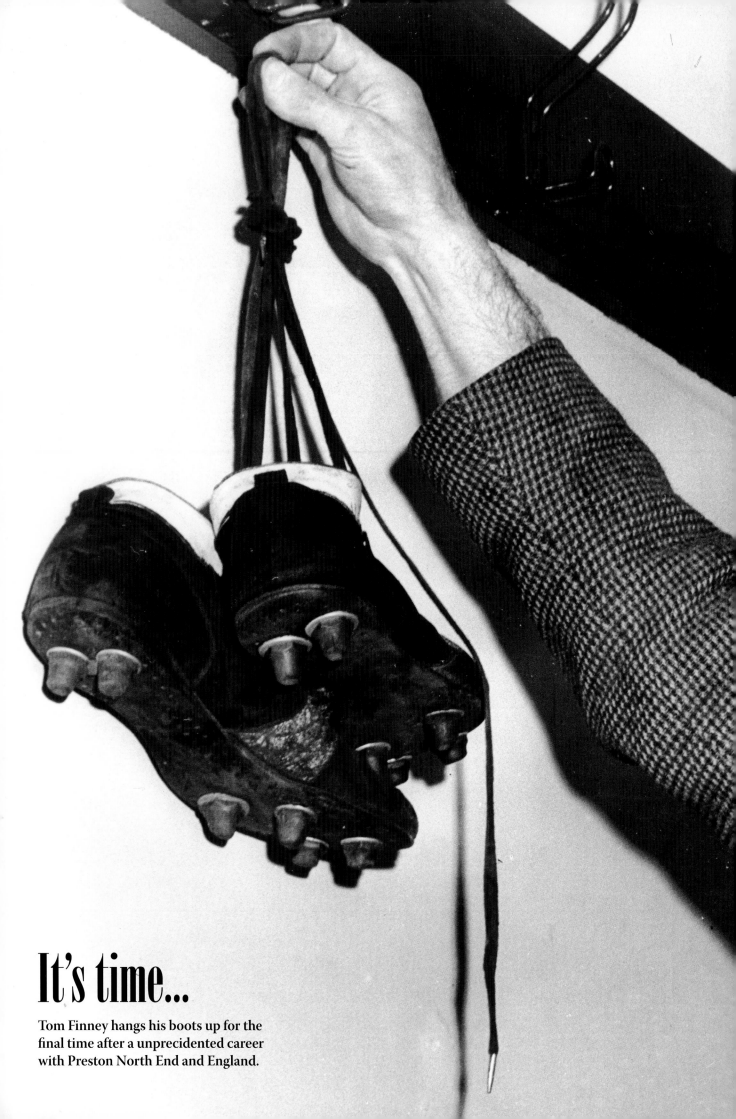

It's time...

Tom Finney hangs his boots up for the
final time after a unprecidented career
with Preston North End and England.

Lady Elsie Finney

I have been deeply touched by the many warm and generous tributes paid to me in this magazine and to be honoured by your peers in this way is a truly humbling experience.

However, compliments can go in two directions and I must thank all of those players, officials, referees and journalists who have helped create for me a life in football that has never fallen short of being truly remarkable.

My domestic life has been an equal joy fuelled by the love of my children Brian and Barbara and grandchildren Donna, Paul, Lee and Lauren.

Finally, I would like to dedicate this magazine and all of the plaudits that I have received to the woman that made my life complete.

Lady Elsie Finney... the love of my life.